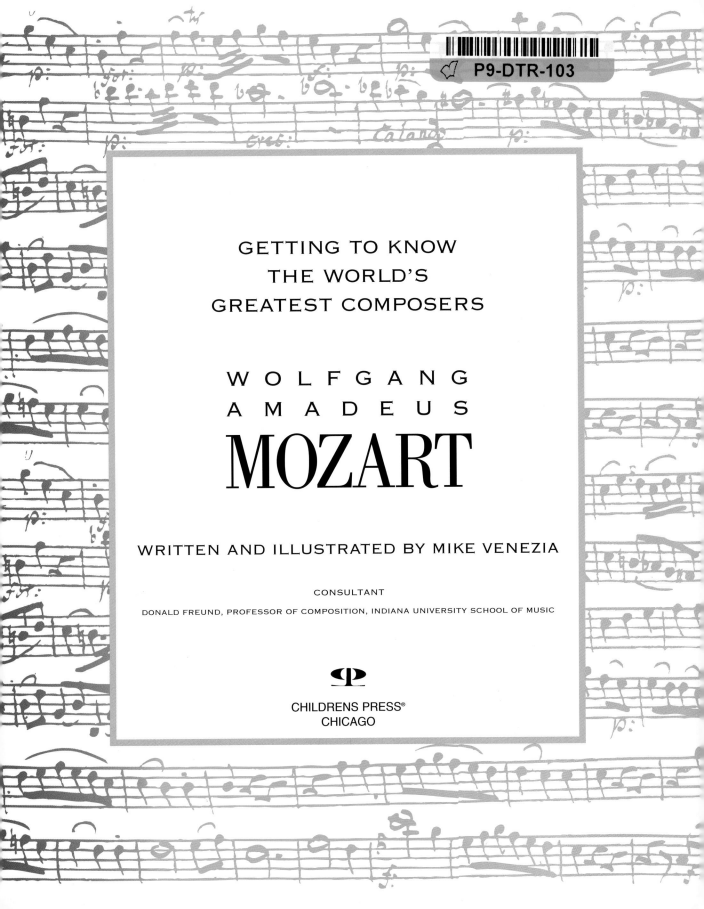

GETTING TO KNOW THE WORLD'S GREATEST COMPOSERS

WOLFGANG AMADEUS MOZART

WRITTEN AND ILLUSTRATED BY MIKE VENEZIA

CONSULTANT

DONALD FREUND, PROFESSOR OF COMPOSITION, INDIANA UNIVERSITY SCHOOL OF MUSIC

CHILDRENS PRESS®
CHICAGO

For Samuel Anthony Venezia
Welcome!

Picture Acknowledgments
Music on the cover, Stock Montage, Inc.; 3, Joseph Lange, oil on canvas, 1789,
© Internationale Stiftung Mozarteum, Salzburg; 7, Michel-Barthelemy Ollivier,
In the Salon of 4 mirrors at the Temple, 1764, Louvre; 8, North Wind Picture
Archives; 9, Bettmann Archives; 13 (both paintings), Pietro Antonio Lorenzoni,
oil on canvas, 1763, © Internationale Stiftung Mozarteum, Salzburg; 16,
J. Dublessis, Louvre; 19, Bettmann Archive; 21, Anonymous, oil on canvas,
© Internationale Stiftung Mozarteum, Salzburg; 24, Bettmann Archive; 25,
North Wind Picture Archives; 26, Hans Hansen, oil on canvas, 1802,
© Internationale Stiftung Mozarteum, Salzburg; 27, 29, AKG London; 30,
Bettmann Archive; 31, San Francisco Opera, Mozart's *Don Giovanni*, 1991,
photo by Marty Sohl; 32, Bettmann Archive

Project Editor: Shari Joffe
Design: PCI Design Group, San Antonio, Texas
Photo Research: Jan Izzo

Library of Congress Cataloging–in–Publication Data

Venezia, Mike.
    Wolfgang Amadeus Mozart / written and illustrated by Mike Venezia.
    p.   cm. -- (Getting to know the world's greatest composers)
    Summary: A biography of the child prodigy who wrote more than 800
    pieces of music before his untimely death at thirty-five.
    ISBN 0-516-04541-5 (lib. bdg.)—ISBN 0-516-44541-3 (pbk.)
    1. Mozart, Wolfgang Amadeus, 1756-1791--Juvenile literature.
    2. Composers--Austria--Biography--Juvenile literature.
    [1. Mozart, Wolfgang Amadeus, 1756-1791. 2. Composers.]
    I. Title. II. Series: Venezia, Mike.
    Getting to know the world's greatest composers.
    ML3930.M9V46   1995
    780' .92--dc20
    [B]   95-13366
                                                               CIP
                                                               AC

    16 R 10 09 08   62

A portrait of Wolfgang Amadeus Mozart at about age 33

Wolfgang Amadeus Mozart was born in Salzburg, Austria, in 1756. Many people think he was the greatest composer who ever lived. Even though Mozart's music was very popular during his time, he often had to struggle just to make a living.

The type of music that Wolfgang Amadeus Mozart played and composed is known as classical music. It was usually written for an occasion like an emperor's court dance or a princess's wedding, or a special church occasion, or an opera. Royal families and other wealthy people who hired composers

and musicians were known as patrons.

Many of these wealthy people loved
being entertained by music so much
that they even had their own orchestras!
Unfortunately, most patrons thought
of musicians as servants, no matter
how talented they were, and paid them
very little money.

Classical music in the 1700s had to follow certain rules to be acceptable in the palaces and royal courts of Europe. Even though people loved to be entertained by music, they didn't like many surprises. They expected to hear familiar forms of music, like symphonies, concertos, or sonatas. For royal dances, the music had to be light and happy. For background music at a gathering, it had to be clear and simple, and not too loud. No one wanted it to get in the way of their conversations. Because of these rules, some classical music sounded controlled and not very interesting.

Wolfgang, age ten, performing for French royalty in Paris in 1766

Great composers like Mozart, however, were able to follow the rules of classical music and create musical masterpieces. They experimented and found ways to put their personal feelings of love, sadness, or fun into classical music and make it very exciting and beautiful.

Wolfgang Amadeus Mozart had quite a remarkable childhood. He and his sister, Nannerl, who was four years older, traveled all over with their parents, playing music for the royal families of Europe. Wolfgang's father, Leopold Mozart, was a composer and violinist in the court of the prince-archbishop of Salzburg.

Mr. Mozart was happily surprised to find that his daughter had a special talent when he began giving her clavier lessons. A clavier is a keyboard instrument similar to a piano. Nannerl quickly learned to play the most difficult pieces.

Mr. Mozart was *really* surprised,
though, when he noticed Wolfgang trying
to play the same pieces Nannerl had been
practicing. When he was only three years
old, Wolfgang Amadeus Mozart already
had an unusual understanding of music.
When he was four, he learned to play the
violin perfectly!

And when he was six years old, Wolfgang wrote a concerto, a difficult musical form even for an experienced grown-up to write. Mr. and Mrs. Mozart soon realized Wolfgang and Nannerl were different from other children.

In 1762, when Wolfgang was six and Nannerl was ten, Mr. Mozart decided it was time to travel and show his talented children to the world.

Trips during this time
were very difficult—and even
dangerous! Sometimes coaches
could travel only a few miles
a day because of breakdowns
or bumpy, rut-filled roads.

It was cold much of the time, and the inns where the Mozarts stayed at night were uncomfortable. Fortunately, Wolfgang and Nannerl loved performing for audiences so much that they never seemed to mind.

Wolfgang at age six

They also enjoyed seeing the great cities of Europe, like Vienna, Paris, London, Prague, and Munich.

Nannerl at age eleven

Some people thought Mr. Mozart was taking advantage of his children by making them work hard for money. But Leopold Mozart was a good father who really loved his children and was concerned about their future. He felt that if Wolfgang and Nannerl became famous at an early age, they would have a better chance of making livings as musicians when they grew up.

Making enough money was always a problem for the Mozarts.

Even when audiences went wild over their performances, the Mozart children were often paid with gifts. What Mr. Mozart really needed was money to pay for coaches, hotels, clothing, and food.

During his many journeys, Wolfgang wrote lots of new pieces and learned about the music of other countries. In London, England, he studied the music of the great composer George Frideric Handel. In Germany, he learned about mixing different tunes into the same piece of music. This is called *counterpoint.*

Everything was going well, but then something happened. In 1768, Wolfgang was asked to compose and conduct an opera in Vienna for the Emperor Joseph II.

A portrait that suggests Mozart at about age twelve

For some reason, the emperor's musicians started to give Wolfgang a hard time. They may have been jealous, or afraid they would look bad, being directed by a twelve-year-old boy. They caused so many annoying problems that Mr. Mozart gave up trying to put the opera together, and took Wolfgang home to Salzburg.

Another problem was that Wolfgang and Nannerl were growing up. People didn't find them quite as cute and remarkable as they once had. Wolfgang knew he would have to amaze people now by writing and playing the best music ever—which is just what he did.

In 1769, Mr. Mozart thought it would be a good idea to take one more trip. This time, just he and Wolfgang would go to Italy.

Nannerl, Wolfgang, and Leopold Mozart

It was decided that Nannerl would stay home with her mother.

Italy was the most important music center of Europe. In Rome, Florence, Naples, and Venice, Wolfgang saw the great Italian operas and heard the clear, delicate melodies of the Italian musical style. Mr. Mozart thought he might be able to get Wolfgang a position in an important Italian court, but it never worked out.

r. Mozart really involved himself in Wolfgang's life, and spent lots of time trying to get the best job he could for his son. Leopold Mozart meant well, but didn't give Wolfgang much of a chance to do anything on his own. When they returned home from Italy, Wolfgang was able to get a job with his father in the archbishop's court orchestra. Things were OK until a new archbishop took over.

Archbishop Heironymous Colloredo never appreciated Wolfgang Mozart's wonderful talent. He was often rude to Wolfgang, and ordered him to write all kinds of boring musical pieces, sometimes at the last minute.

Wolfgang was very unhappy during this time. Much to his father's disappointment, he wanted to quit his job and travel to kingdoms and cities where he had been a big hit as a child.

Wolfgang really wanted to have the freedom to find his own jobs and make his own decisions about what kind of music he would write and play. Mr. Mozart finally agreed that Wolfgang could go on the trip if his mother went along too. Mr. Mozart wanted his wife to keep an eye on their son, to make sure he didn't waste all his money.

Wolfgang Amadeus Mozart was able to compose and perform some of the greatest music ever, but when it came to handling money, he didn't do very well. Wolfgang loved to spend money by giving parties, going on dates, and buying expensive clothing and wigs. He also loved playing games of all kinds, such as billiards and lawn bowling.

Anna Maria Mozart, Wolfgang's mother

In some of the cities that Wolfgang visited, he continued to amaze audiences. But in other cities, no one seemed to care that much about his music anymore. Wolfgang was becoming upset. In Paris, the worst thing of all happened. Mrs. Mozart became ill, and after a short time, died. Wolfgang was deeply saddened, and returned home to Salzburg.

By the time he got there, Mr. Mozart had talked the archbishop into giving Wolfgang a job as court organist. The new job didn't last very long, though. Wolfgang and the archbishop still had big problems getting along. After a huge argument, the archbishop had Wolfgang kicked out of his palace!

Wolfgang's home in Salzburg

In 1779, Wolfgang Mozart left Salzburg for good. He decided to go to Vienna, a city where he had lots of friends. Even though the emperor's musicians had given him some problems a few years earlier, Wolfgang knew that Joseph II really appreciated his music.

It was in Vienna that Wolfgang fell in love, and married a singer named Constanze Weber. Wolfgang had some of the happiest times of his life in Vienna and wrote many of his greatest works. But as time went on, Wolfgang got himself into money problems again.

Wolfgang's wife, Constanze Mozart

He often had to work day and night to put on concerts and write music for special occasions. Even with Constanze's help and encouragement, Wolfgang Mozart's health started getting worse and worse.

Some people feel that Wolfgang Mozart's most important musical achievement was his operas. After he moved to Vienna, Wolfgang wrote some of his greatest operas, like *The Marriage of Figaro, Don Giovanni,* and *The Magic Flute.*

During this time, there were two main types of operas. Serious ones, with stories about kings, gods, and heroes, were called *opera seria.* Funny ones about everyday people were called *opera buffa.* Wolfgang did an amazing thing by sometimes mixing these different styles in the same opera! He made his operas more interesting by showing that—as in real life—things aren't always just serious or just funny.

A set design for a scene from Mozart's opera *The Magic Flute*

In one of his most popular operas, *The Magic Flute*, Mozart combined all kinds of musical moods. There is the frightening, powerful music he wrote for the wise sorcerer, Sarastro, who sings some of the lowest and most serious notes ever. In another piece, the evil Queen of the Night sings some of the highest and fastest notes you'll ever hear!

Papageno, a character
from *The Magic Flute*

Then there are
the love songs that
Prince Tamino and
Princess Pamina
sing to each other.
Finally, there is the playful
music written for the comedy
characters Papageno
the bird catcher and
his girlfriend Papagena.

In one part, Mozart has
them sing their names back and
forth so quickly that they sound almost
like an unusual instrument, especially
the "Pa-Pa-Pa-Pa-Pa . . ." part. It's
so much fun to listen to, you might
find yourself trying to sing along to
see if you can keep up with Papageno
and Papagena.

One of the greatest things Wolfgang Mozart was able to do in his operas was create music that gives you such a clear understanding of each character that you feel you almost know them, or know a lot about them.

A scene from Mozart's opera *Don Giovanni*

Mozart composing the *Requiem* from his deathbed

After he finished *The Magic Flute*, Wolfgang Amadeus Mozart wasn't well at all. He used all the energy he had to compose a piece called *Requiem*, but died before he could finish it. Wolfgang was only 35 years old.

Wolfgang Amadeus Mozart wrote more than 800 pieces of music. It's usually hard for people to choose a favorite one, because so many of them are wonderful to listen to. Almost all of Mozart's music seems to have a mysterious power and beauty to it. It's easy to find Mozart's music on the radio, or on cassette tapes and compact discs at your local library.